# DROPPING THE WEIGHTS

# DROPPING THE WEIGHTS

## THE ROAD TO INTENTION

MARK D CARROLL

XULON PRESS

Xulon Press
555 Winderley Pl, Suite 225
Maitland, FL 32751
407.339.4217
www.xulonpress.com

Paperback ISBN-13: 978-1-66289-425-1
eBook ISBN-13: 97-81-66289-426-8

I first like to Dedicate this New Book God put on my heart to write, To Him, because without Him this book and others to come would not be possible. Also, to my beautiful wife and our two adult kids, who have always been my BIGGEST supporters and encouraged me to keep going no matter what! And a Special THANKS to my business partner and great friend Kasey Yale who helped me with the pre-editing of this book. My Dream is that whoever reads this book will come away with a Newfound way thinking of oneself and having the confidence to walk it out knowing that you don't have to Carry unnecessary Weights of life. So, let's ALL walk with a New Focused Intention and say, "I AM NO LONGER MY SHAME, PAIN, or PAST" I Can Drop It!

# CONTENTS

 # WEIGHT #1

## ANGER

The physical effects of anger include an increase in heart rate, blood pressure, and levels of adrenaline and noradrenaline (also known as norepinephrine).

According to Harvard Health and NIH (National Institutes of Health 2012), people view anger as part of the fight or flight response that the brain uses for perceived threat of harm.

In my own life, I have seen how anger can have several physical and mental consequences, such as:

1) A decrease in productivity
2) An increase in job stress
3) Health problems

**Cause**: Lack of control

**Cure**: Walking by the Spirit, Trusting God, forgiving others and self, mercy, and patience

**Scripture**:

Psalm 4:4) The Bible says, "Be angry, but don't sin."

**Meaning**:

It's okay to be angry, but it's going to be your words that determine whether or not a "pride wall" will go up for the person listening.

Pray for peace to get your anger out.

**How…?**

Three Practical Steps:

1) ***Acknowledge*** you have it by writing it out (or confessing it out loud)
2) ***Tear it out!***
3) ***Throw it out!***

 # WEIGHT #2

## UNFORGIVENESS

The golden rule is widely understood to be, "Do unto others as you would have them do also to you." In the world today, however due to the glorification of selfishness and a misunderstanding of reconciliation, people use the term "unforgiveness" as literally "good."

World studies show that a neurotic personality is less likely to forgive or to have a disposition of forgiveness. (Sciencedirect.com 2007) says, "Highly agreeable and extraverted individuals have been found to be more likely to forgive. People who score high on Neuroticism and related affective traits of anger, chronic hostility, anxiety, and depression have been found to be less likely to forgive." Generally, the offended person looks for and waits to see sincerity and remorse for the offense.

The Bible, however, says that the Christian's "sin debt" (the price we owed but Jesus paid) to God should be motivation enough to forgive all who have done or said wrong things to us.

**Cause**: Bitterness

**Cure**: Walking by the Spirit, love for God and others from the heart

**Scripture**:

> Then Peter came up and said to him, "Lord, how often will my brother sin against me, and I forgive him? As many as seven times?" Jesus said to him, "I do not say to you seven times, but seventy-seven times. (Matt. 18:21-35)

**Meaning**:

Don't seek revenge yourself - but give place to God's wrath.

> "For it is written, 'Vengeance belongs to Me, I will Repay,' says the Lord." (Romans 12:19)

**How...?**

Three Practical Steps:

1) **Write** (or confess) your unforgiveness out!
2) **Pray** your unforgiveness out!

Then...

3) **Throw it out!**

# WEIGHT #3

## PRIDE/ FALSE HUMILITY

Pride robs you of being who God created you to be. When looked at, pride is a VIRTUE or VICE. It can be viewed as pride in one's appearance and abilities, which is known as virtuous pride, greatness of soul, or magnanimity. But as a "weight," it's viewed as a vice and is often termed "vanity" or "vainglory."

As we all know, most world religions do consider "pride" a sin. Pride, in this sense of being "sinful," is knowing you're wrong but refusing to admit it. Also, it is assuming you know the outcome of the future without knowing it. This is a pride called "arrogance."

**Cause:** Thinking we are special above God or others

**Cure**: Walking by the Spirit, Putting God, and others first

**Scripture**:

> "You ought to say, 'If it be the Lord's Will, we shall live and do this or that'" (James 4:15).

**Meaning**:

Facing up to the truth will always produce a loss of some kind.

In other words, admit it (to yourself) and quit it!

**How…?**

Three Practical Steps:

1) **Write** (or confess) your pride OUT!
2) **Pray** your pride OUT!

Then…

3) **Throw it Out!**

 # WEIGHT #4

## SELFISHNESS

When you have confusion and evil dealing, you have selfish ambitions. Some have argued that you can equate selfishness with the act of self-serving, but we all know that selfishness implies the intention to serve only yourself. Just so that we're all crystal clear here, Selfishness is the exact opposite of selflessness.

**Cause:** Lack of regard for others

**Cure**: Walking by the spirit, love for others

**Scripture:** says:

> "Let each of you look out not only for his own interests, but also for the interests of others" (Phil. 2:4).

**Meaning**:

Selfishness basically defies all sound judgment.

**How...?**

Three Practical Steps:

1) **Write** (or confess) selfishness out
2) **Pray** selfishness out!

Then ...

3) **Throw it Out**!

# WEIGHT #5

## DOUBT

Doubt is basically like emotional blackmail, but it's all self-inflicted. Oftentimes, it tends to call on our own limited reasoning. It also encourages people to hesitate before acting and leads toward disbelief or non-acceptance. Doctors, at times, consider doubt as a symptom of a possible phobia, deriving from when the ego is developed.

According to (OpenText, 2014) "Freud proposed that we use defense mechanisms to cope with anxiety and maintain a positive self-image."

Perhaps we can concur that negative early childhood experiences and ill spirited traditions can cause doubt in one's abilities and even about one's very own identity.

**Cause**: A lack of faith

**Cure**: Walk by the Spirit, Trust in God and believe He loves you

**Scripture** says, "

> I desire therefore that the men in every place pray, lifting up holy hands without anger and doubting" (1 Tim. 2:8).

Also,

> "But let him ask in faith, without any doubting. For he who doubts is like a wave of the sea, driven by the wind and tossed back and forth" (James 1:6).

**Meaning**: Doubt sabotages good things!

**How...?**

Three Practical Steps:

1) **Write** (or confess) doubt out!
2) **Pray** doubt out!

Then ...

3) **Throw it out**!

# WEIGHT #6

## WORRY

Worry is the state of having chains of thoughts of a negative and uncontrollable nature, usually threatening survival. Worry refers to negative self-talk that usually distracts the mind from focusing on the solution to the problem. Worrying can also be harmful for your health, both mentally and physically.

Worrying triggers anxiety or concerns about real or imagined situations like finances, marriage, kids, friends, and the list goes on.

According to (Hopkinsmedicine.org, 2015), "Worrying can also be the main component of generalized anxiety disorder."

**Cause:** A lack of trust

**Cure**: Walk by the spirit. A couple simpler ways to combat worry are things like talking to a friend and eating healthy. Friends can help us have a different perspective when we worry, and survival gets clouded when we are hungry!

Today, see the positive

**Scripture** says, in Luke 12:22,

> "Therefore I say to you, do not worry at all about your life, what you will eat; nor about your body, what you will put on."

**Meaning**: Worry always makes things worse and delays the process!

**How…?**

Three Practical Steps:

1) *Write* (or confess) worry out!
2) *Pray* worry out!

Then…

3) *Throw it out*!

 # WEIGHT #7

## FEAR

There's only one thing we all should have a healthy fear of and that's God! Anything else is just a figment (believed to be real but not) of your imagination like fear of dogs, spiders, heights, water, enclosed spaces, failure, people, bridges, clowns, death, flying, intimacy, rejection, snakes, success, driving, and more. Although the fear we can experience from these things is very real and it can even affect how we physically feel...

**Cause:** A removal of certainty or love

**Cure:** Walk by the Spirit, Love

**Scripture** says,

> "For He did not give you a spirit of fear, but of power, love, and a sound mind" (2 Tim. 1:7).

**Meaning**:

Fear is an emotional response to an imaginary perceived threat, but the key is to remember God's love for us. So, let Him lead.

**How...?**

Three Practical Steps:

1) *Write* (or confess) fear out!
2) *Pray* fear out!

Then...

3) *Throw it out*!

# 🏋 WEIGHT #8

## CONFUSION

Confusion is usually an inability to focus on a task and can often cause an inability to get along with others. It can also be a symptom of mental and physical problems and can range from mild to severe (Healthdirect.gov ND).

**Cause**: Lack of perception

**Cure**: Sleep, rest, food, prayer, and sobriety

**Scripture**:

We do not have a spirit of confusion

"For where jealousy and selfish ambition exist, there will be disorder and every vile practice" (James 3:16).

**Meaning**:

When things are not in order, people are scared or mean and often, directionless.

**How…?**

Three Practical Steps:

1) *Write* (or confess) confusion out!
2) *Pray* confusion out!

Then …

3) *Throw it out*!

#  WEIGHT #9

## DISCOURAGEMENT

Discouragement basically means to dishearten by expressing disapproval or by suggesting to a person that a contemplated action or course will pretty much fail (Dictionary.com, ND). It also means to intimidate, to drive courage or confidence, or to hinder by disfavoring the person.

**Cause:** Listening to doubt from self or others

**Cure:** Believe there can be good things despite the doubt.

**Scripture**:

> "Be not discouraged, For I the Lord have overcome the world (John 16:33).

**Meaning**:

Discouragement can keep us from achieving great things if we listen to negative words!

**How…?**

Three Practical Steps:

1) ***Write*** (or confess) discouragement!
2) ***Pray*** discouragement out!

Then…

3) ***Throw it out***!

 # WEIGHT #10

## DEPRESSION

"Depression is a psychotic disorder marked especially by sadness, inactivity, difficulty in thinking and concentration, a significant increase or decrease in appetite and time spent sleeping, feelings of dejection and hopelessness, and sometimes, suicidal tendencies" (Brittanica.com, ND).

**Cause**: Loneliness, negative thinking

**Cure**: Time with the with God is key to your rest!

**Scripture**: Psalm 18 says,

"The Lord is my rock and my fortress and my deliverer; my shield and the horn of my salvation, my stronghold," (against depression). "In my distress, I called upon the Lord."

"He hears me!"

**Meaning:** If we talk to god about what is keeping us depressed, he will walk us through it.

**How…?**

Three Practical Steps:

1) *Write* (or confess) depression out!
2) *Pray* depression out!

Then …

3) *Throw it out*!

# WEIGHT #11

## LUST

Lusts are objects of desire. It's a personal inclination, an intense or unbridled physical, mental, or sexual desire, or an intense longing or craving, which could lead to violence.

> "Each person is tempted when they are drawn away by their own lust and enticed." Then comes sin, then death" (James 1:14).

The lust is the attractive trap that brings destruction or calamity.

**Cause**: An unwillingness to turn away from our will or desire, prioritizing desire over God

**Cure**: Scripture warns us how to *identify* and *resist* lust.

**Scripture**:

> "Therefore, submit to God. Resist the devil and he will flee from you. Draw near to God and He will draw near to you" (James 4:7-8).

> "Therefore, lay aside all filthiness and overflow of wickedness, and receive with meekness the implanted word which is able to save your souls" (James 1:21).

**Meaning: Run from lust!!!**

**How…?**

Three Practical Steps:

1) ***Write*** (or confess) your lust out!
2) ***Pray*** your lust out!

Then …

3) ***Throw it out!***

# WEIGHT #12

## LYING

Lying is simply not telling the truth about something. "A lie is an "untrue statement." (Merriam Webster.com, ND)

There's no such thing as a "little white lie" or "half-truths." A lie is a lie— period!

To tell someone a lie is regarded as inflicting a mental injury on oneself and on that person. According to an online article, maintaining false facts hurts our brain in the long run! (snexplores, 2022)

**Cause**: Disdain for truth, Selfishness, fear, greed

**Cure**: Walk by the Spirit, Tell the truth, and trust God with the consequences

**Scripture**:

> "Just put away lying, let each one of us speak truth with everyone. Let no corrupt word proceed out of your mouth, but what is good for necessary edification, that it may impart grace to the hearer" (Eph. 4: 25- 29).

**Meaning**: Just tell the truth!

**How…?**

Three Practical Steps:

1) ***Write*** (or confess) your "lie!"
2) ***Pray*** your "lie" out!

Then …

3) ***Throw it out***!

 # WEIGHT #13

## ADULTERY

Adultery, whether doing the act or even thinking about the act, is a sin (Matt. 5:28). God sees it the same as extramarital sex. It's sexual infidelity to your spouse because it's done in the heart.

In some countries in the Middle East, like Saudi Arabia, and some states in the US, it is illegal and considered a serious offense (Lawstackexchange 2022). In some cases, it's punishable by death or dismemberment.

**Cause**: Impulse, greed, and selfishness.

**Cure**: Self-control, Love, Devotion to God and Spouse

**Scripture**:

"As far as the east is from the west, so far has he removed all of our transgressions from us" (Ps. 103:12).

"Flee sexual immorality, every sin that a man does is outside the body, but he who commits sexual immorality sins against his own body" (1 Cor. 6:18).

"No adulterer will inherit the kingdom." (1 Cor.9-11)

**Meaning:** Tend to your own home

**How...?**

Three Practical Steps:

1) ***Write*** (or confess) your adultery out!
2) ***Pray*** your adultery out!

Then...

3) ***Throw it out***!

# WEIGHT #14

## SEXUAL IMMORALITY

Biblically, sexual immorality is being led by unnatural sexual desires that decrease our desire for holiness and increase our desire for people and things in the world.

**Cause**: Long looks, lingering thoughts, pornography, sexual related themes, disobedience

**Cure**: Walking by the Spirit, Abstinence and fleeing sexual situations and conversations

**Scripture**:

"Do not keep company with sexually immoral people" (1 Cor. 5:9).

"So, I Say, Walk by the spirit and you will not fulfill the desires of the flesh" (Gal. 5:16).

**Meaning**:

**How...?**

Three Practical Steps:

1) **Write** (or confess) your sexual tie out!
2) **Pray** your sexual tie out!

Then ...

3) **Throw it out!**

 # WEIGHT #15

## STRESS

Stress is a normal physical response to an event that makes you feel threatened or upsets your balance in some way. Whenever you sense danger, whether it's real or imagined, the body's defenses kick into high gear in a rapid, automatic process known as "the fight or flight" reaction or the stress response (Rx outreach, ND).

Stress can help you rise to meet challenges, such as slamming on your brakes to avoid an accident. It also sharpens your concentration.

**Cause**: Reacting vs responding.

**Cure**: Relax (i.e., read a book, take a walk, etc.).

**Scripture**:

"Come to me, all you who labor and are heavy stressed, and I will give you rest" (Matt. 11:28- 30; John 14:27).

**Meaning**:

**How...?**

Three Practical Steps:

1) **Write** your stress out!
2) **Pray** your stress out!

Then ...

3) **Throw it out**!

# WEIGHT #16

## ARROGANCE

(Dictionary.com, ND) defines arrogance as having or revealing an exaggerated sense of one's own importance or abilities. Arrogant people often try to hide a lot of pain (wikihow.com, ND). In my experience, at some point or another, arrogant people realize that the world doesn't revolve around them. They counteract this by creating an atmosphere that centers around them and get angry or bothered if they're reminded of the real world.

Arrogant people have a strong need to look good. When you make them look bad, even if it's the slightest offense, they will usually be very mad at you. This happens when you question (or at least seem to question) their appearance, intelligence, athletic ability, or anything else relating to their self-image or lifestyle.

**Cause**: Hardened heart

**Cure**: Humility

**Scripture**:

> "You boast in your arrogance, all such boasting is Evil..." (James 4:16). "A proud and haughty man - "Scoffer" is his name: He acts with arrogant pride" (Prov. 21:24).

**Meaning**:

**How...?**

Three Practical Steps:

1) **Write** your arrogance out!
2) **Pray** your arrogance out!

Then...

3) **Throw it out**!

 # WEIGHT #17

## ANXIETY

Anxiety occurs when you're experiencing worry, unease, or nervousness, typically about an event or something with an uncertain or unknown outcome.

This is when we become concerned, disturbed, or apprehensive, causing anxiety. (Medlineplus, ND)

It can also be caused by wanting something or someone so badly that one feels they can't be patient. Further, this is a relatively permanent state of worry and nervousness, occurring in a variety of mental disorders and usually accompanied by compulsive behavior or attacks of panic.

**Cause**: A paradigm imbalance, which is a skewed or shifting perception of reality based on what could be rather than what is.

**Cure**: Tell God the anxieties

**Scripture**:

"Be anxious for nothing, but in everything by prayer and supplication with thanksgivings, let your requests be made known to God; And the peace of God, which surpasses all understanding, will guard your hearts and minds through Christ Jesus" (Phil. 4:6- 7).

**Meaning**:

**How…?**

Three Practical Steps:

1) *Write* (or confess) your "anxiousness" out!
2) *Pray* your "anxiousness" out!

Then …

3) *Throw it out*!

 # WEIGHT #18

## BITTERNESS

Bitterness is "a feeling of anger and disappointment at being treated unfairly" (Oxford learners dictionary, ND).

Unresolved bitterness can spawn an array of serious problems, such as depression, insomnia, emotional instability, rage, and outbursts. Such stress can also exacerbate cardiovascular problems.

Especially in cases where others show little or no gratitude at all, you focus on what that person has done to you. You keep a filing cabinet with their name on it and replay everything they have done to you in your mind. This often causes a stubborn or sulking attitude.

**Cause**: Flesh

**Cure**: Gratitude, Love

**Scripture**:

> "Pursue peace with all people, and holiness, without which no one will see the Lord. Looking carefully lest anyone fall short of the grace of God; Lest any root of bitterness springing up come trouble, and by this many become defiled" (Heb. 12:24).

**Meaning**:

**How...?**

Three Practical Steps:

1    )***Write*** your bitterness out!
2)  ***Pray*** your bitterness out!

Then…

3)  ***Throw it out***!

# WEIGHT #19

## DECEPTION

Deception is basically intentionally managing verbal and/or nonverbal messages so that the receiver will believe in a way that the message sender knows is false. (law.cornell.edu, 2021).

It can also employ distraction, camouflage, or concealment.

There is also self-deception, a convenient trick of the flesh to feel better about doing the wrong thing.

**Cause**: Self-interest

**Cure**: Love of truth

**Scripture**:

> "You must renounce secret and shameful ways: we do not use deception, nor do we distort the word of God. On the contrary, by setting forth the truth plainly we commend ourselves to everyone's conscience in the sight of God" (2 Cor. 4:2).

All deception is evil and not of God.

**Meaning**:

**How…?**

Three Practical Steps:

    1)   ***Write*** (or confess) your deception out!
    2)   ***Pray*** your deception out!

Then …

    3*)*   ***Throw it out***!

# 🔔 WEIGHT #20

## GREED

Biblically, greed is the seventh of the deadly sins.

Also, it's an excessive desire to possess wealth or goods and is also known as "covetousness." Like lust and gluttony, it's a sin of excess.

Greed is an inappropriate expectation. It's a sin against God, just as all mortal sins. Other actions inspired by greed are disloyalty, deliberate betrayal, or treason, especially for personal gain through bribery, trickery, or manipulation of authority.

As a secular psychological concept, greed is an inordinate desire to acquire or possess more than one needs or deserves, especially with respect to material wealth

(Thefreedictionary.com, 2014).

**Cause**: Thoughtlessness for others.

**Cure**: Placing others needs above own

**Scripture**:

> "The greedy bring ruin to their households, but the one who hates bribes will live" (Prov. 15:27). "The greedy store up conflict, but those who trust in the Lord will prosper" (Prov. 28:25).

**Meaning**:

**How…?**

Three Practical Steps:

1) **Write** your greed out!
2) **Pray** your greed out!

Then…

3) **Throw it out**!

 # WEIGHT #21

## IDOLATRY

Idolatry is the religious worship of idols, excessive or blind adoration, reverence, devotion, etc. (Dictionary.com, ND).

This is usually defined as worship of any cult image, idea, or object, as if it were God (Britannica.com, ND).

An idol is anything that replaces the one true God.

From personal experience, we may not realize we have set up idols in our lives until God asks us to prioritize Him over that thing.

**Cause**: Flesh.

**Cure**: Love God with all your heart

**Scripture**:

> "You shall have no other gods before me" (Exod. 20:3-4). "Walk by the spirit and you will not fulfill the desires of the flesh" (Gal. 5).

> "Flee from idolatry" (1 Cor. 10:14).

**Meaning**:

**How...?**

Three Practical Steps:

1) ***Write*** your idolatry out!
2) ***Pray*** your idolatry out!

Then…

3) ***Throw it out***!

# ⚖ WEIGHT #22

## CURSING

(Dictionary.com, ND) says cursing is a profane or obscene expression of anger, disgust, or surprise directed at someone or something. Also, cursing is something that causes great trouble or harm by invoking evil or misfortune upon another to inflict pain or decide they are less than us.

Profanity is a word, expression, gesture, or other social behavior, which is socially constructed or interpreted as insulting, rude, vulgar, desecrating, or disrespectful.

**Cause**: Fear, impulse, hurt, and anger

**Cure**: Walk by the Spirit, Stop saying them

**Scripture**:

> "Let NO, Corrupt word proceed out of your mouth, but what is good for necessary edification, that it may impart GRACE to the hearer"

> "Let all bitterness, wrath, anger, clamor and evil speaking be put away from you, with all malice" (Eph. 4: 29-31).

> "But NO man can tame the tongue. It's an Unruly evil, full of deadly poison. With it, we bless our God and Father and with it we curse men, who have been made in the similitude of God" (James 3:8-10).

**Meaning**: Keep watch over your mouth

**How…?**

Three Practical Steps:

1) **Write** your profanity out!
2) **Pray** your profanity out!

Then …

3) **Throw it out!**

# WEIGHT #23

## STEALING

Stealing is defined as an unauthorized taking, keeping, or using of another's property without permission.

**Cause**: Psychological

**Cure**: Respect and love for others

**Scripture**:

"You shall not steal" (Exod. 20:15).

> "Anyone who has been stealing must steal no longer, but must work, doing something useful with their own hands, that they may have something to share with those in need" (Eph. 4:28).

**How…?**

**Meaning:** Don't take what's not yours.

Three Practical Steps:

1) *Write* your stealing out!
2) *Pray* your stealing out!

Then…

3) *Throw it out*!

# ⬤ WEIGHT #24

## JUDGING

Whenever a person judges, they have already formed an opinion.

The Bible states clearly that we should never judge anyone unless you're in an authority position where discernment is involved!

Compassion, love, and understanding of the whole picture with wisdom is needed to judge righteously.

Any lazy, biased, uncaring, and unthinking fool can have an opinion or judgment about you. So, before you open your mouth to judge someone, use TLC.

Whatever measure you use in judging others, it will be used to measure how you are judged.

**Cause**: Flesh and disobedience

**Cure**: Walk by the Spirit, Grace, intercession, patience, humility

**Scripture**:

"Judge not, lest you be judged." (Matthew 7:1-3)

For judgment will be merciless to one who has shown no mercy; but (to the one who has shown mercy) mercy triumphs (victoriously) over judgment. (James 2:13).

**Meaning**: Righteous judgement only comes from God.

**How so...?**

Three Practical Steps:

1) **Write** your judging out!
2) **Pray** your judging out!

Then …

3) **Throw it out**!

 # WEIGHT #25

## COMPLAINING

Complaining is not mere observation; it is a creative act. The more you complain, the more you summon your creative energies to attract something to complain about.

Your complaints may seem fully justified, but realize that, whenever you complain, you are planning your order for more of the same.

Complaining is not merely about the past. Whenever you make a complaint, realize you are setting an intention or a goal for the future.

**Cause**: Unsatisfied flesh.

**Cure**: Walk by the Spirit, Finding contentment in The Lord

**Scripture**:

> "Why should a living man complain- let us search out and examine our ways and turn back to God" (Lam. 3: 39-:40).

> "Do all things without complaining and disputing, that you may become blameless and harmless, children of God without fault in the midst of a crooked and perverse generation" (Phil. 2:14-15).

**Meaning**: Delay has a purpose

**How…?**

Three Practical Steps:

1) ***Write*** your complaint out!
2) ***Pray*** your complaint out!

Then...

3) ***Throw it out***!

# WEIGHT #26

## IMMATURITY

(Merriam Webster, ND) defines "immaturity" as "exhibiting less than an expected degree of maturity."

Immaturity is the unwillingness to recognize that it often reflects the learned control a person displays toward the stresses of pre and post adulthood. Immaturity is also exercised over impulsivity, inappropriate responses, and an unwillingness to compromise. So, in other words, GROW UP.

**Cause**: Lack of growth.

**Cure:** Walk by the Spirit, Seek the Lord for truth and growth.

**Scripture**:

> We have much to say about this, but it is hard to make clear to you because you no longer try to understand. In fact, though by this time you ought to be teachers, you need someone to teach you the elementary truths of God's Word all over again. You need milk, not solid food! (Heb. 5: 11-14).

**Meaning**: Be willing to listen and hear

**How…?**

Three Practical Steps:

1) *Write* (or confess) your immaturity out!
2) *Pray* your immaturity out!

Then …

3) *Throw It Out!*

# WEIGHT #27

## OPPRESSION

Oppression is "the exercise of authority or power in a burdensome, cruel, or unjust manner" (Dictionary.com ND) (Merriam webster, ND). It can be defined as an act or instance of oppressing, the state of being oppressed, or the feeling of being heavily burdened, (mentally or physically) by troubles, adverse conditions, or anxiety.

Social Oppression is the systemic, socially supported mistreatment and exploitation of a group or category of people by another (National Institutes of health, ND).

Indirect Oppression is oppression that's affected by psychological attack, situational constraints, or other indirect means (worldpossible.org, ND).

Internalized Oppression- "In sociology and psychology, internalized Oppression is the way an oppressed group comes to use against itself, the methods of the oppressor. (socialsci.libretexts.org ND)

**Cause**: Selfishness

**Cure**: Walk by the Spirit, Compassion

**Scripture**:

"Though an army may encamp against me, my heart shall not fear; Though war may rise up against me, in this I will be confident" (Psalm 27:3)

"No weapon formed against me shall prosper" (Isa. 54:17).

**Meaning**: God will punish the unjust, but if we take vengeance into our own hands' justice will fall short for us and our oppressors.

Three Practical Steps:

1) **Write** your oppression out!
2) **Pray** your oppression out!

Then ...

3) **Throw it out**!

# WEIGHT #28

## GUILT

Based on sites like (psychsource.com, ND) guilt is an emotion that is created by our imagination following an event or perceived event. It's a feeling that comes when you feel you have not done something, or you feel you have done something bad. It is what is generated when you feel unsatisfied with your performance.

**Cause**: Guilt occurs because, deep down in your subconscious, you have become emotionally attached to an event that you feel in some way responsible for. Either you feel that you did something wrong, feel that you didn't do enough, or feel you should have done something.

Now, extreme loads of guilt may cause you to experience high levels of stress, anxiety, and even depression.

**Cure**: Walk by the Spirit, Repentance, Forgiveness, Reconciliation

**Scripture**:

> "When you draw near to God with a sincere heart and with the full assurance that faith brings, having your heart sprinkled to cleanse you from a guilty conscience and having your body washed with pure water" (Heb.10:22-23).

> "There is no condemnation for those who are in Christ Jesus, who walk not according to the flesh but according to the spirit;" (Rom. 8:1-3).

**Meaning**: If we ask God for forgiveness out of true repentance then he will take that feeling of guilt away.

**How...?**

Three Practical Steps:

1) ***Write*** your guilt out!
2) ***Pray*** your guilt out!

Then ...

3) ***Throw it out***!

 # WEIGHT #29

## THE FLESH

Biblically, "In the flesh," is no good thing!

The flesh refers to man's sinful nature. It could be both physical and material. The harder you try to defeat the flesh on your own, the more spectacular your failure.

The flesh is a way of thinking that leads to bad decisions, which lead to failure. Failure comes from making those bad decisions, and those bad decisions come from being in the flesh and letting your physical urges rule over you.

**Cause**: Adam

**Cure**: Walk by the Spirit, Christ

**Scripture**:

"For whoever sows to their flesh will of the flesh reap corruption, but he who sows to the spirit will of the spirit reap everlasting life" (Gal. 6:8).

**Meaning**: We are no longer our flesh (If you have been crucified in Christ)

**How…?**

Three Practical Steps:

1) *Write* "the flesh" out!
2) *Pray* "the flesh" out!

Then …

3) *Throw it out!*

# WEIGHT #30

## DIVORCE

Divorce happens when a man and wife decide that the vows they made before God meant nothing! It's estimated that forty to fifty percent of all marriages have ended in divorce. (Patrellilaw.com, 2022)

First, marriages that ended in divorce lasted about eight years.

Divorce is the final termination of a marital union, canceling the legal duties, responsibilities of the marriage, and dissolving the bonds of matrimony between the couple and God.

**Cause**: Selfishness

**Cure**: Walk by the Spirit, Selflessness

**Scripture**:

> "I tell you that anyone who divorces his wife, except for sexual immorality, and marries another woman commits adultery" (Matt. 19:9).

Whatever God brings together, let no man separate!

**Meaning**: Keep your vows

**How…?**

Three Practical Steps

1) **Write** (or confess) your act or desire for divorce out!
2) **Pray** your thoughts of divorce out!
3) **Throw it out**!

Now **say**: "In Jesus's name, I'm free!"

# WEIGHT #31

## DRUGS

Broadly speaking, a drug is any substance that, when absorbed into the body of a living organism, alters the normal bodily function (Britannica.com, 2023)

Drugs are usually distinguished from indigenous biochemicals by being introduced from outside the organism.

For example, insulin is a hormone that is synthesized in the body. It is called a hormone when it is synthesized by the pancreas inside the body. But if it is introduced into the body from outside, it is called a drug, and if not used correctly, it can kill you and/or get you addicted.

**Cause**: Emotional or physical pain

**Cure**: Walk by the Spirit, Stop and surrender cravings to the Lord in prayer, Break the pattern.

**Scripture**:

"Don't you realize that your body is the temple of the Holy Spirit, who lives in you and was given to you by God? You do not belong to yourself" (1 Cor. 6:18-20).

**Meaning**: Things of the world can and will be deceptive.

**How…?**

Three Practical Steps:

1) **Write** your drug problem out!
2) **Pray** your drug problem out!
3) **Throw it out**! FORGIVEN!

Now **Say** "In Jesus's name, I'm free"!

# NOTES

# NOTES

# NOTES

# NOTES

# NOTES

# NOTES

Printed in the USA
CPSIA information can be obtained
at www.ICGtesting.com
CBHW052022261024
16440CB00008B/135